SUPER SMART
INFORMATION
STRATEGIES

KNOW WHAT TO ASK:

FORMING GREAT RESEARCH QUESTIONS

by Kristin Fontichiaro and Emily Johnson

CHERRY LAKE PUBLISHING • ANN ARBOR, MICHIGAN

12/15

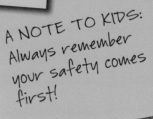

A NOTE TO PARENTS AND TEACHERS: Please remind your children how to stay safe online before they do the activities in this book.

A NOTE TO KIDS: Always remember your safety comes first!

Published in the United States of America
by Cherry Lake Publishing
Ann Arbor, Michigan
www.cherrylakepublishing.com

Content Adviser: Gail Dickinson, PhD,
Associate Professor, Old Dominion University,
Norfolk, Virginia

Photo Credits: Cover, ©Sean Justice/Media Bakery;
page 4, ©Sergiy Nykonenko/Dreamstime.com; page 5,
©Michelle Milliman/Dreamstime.com; page 8, ©Jambostock/Dreamstime.com;
page 11, ©Martin Fischer/Shutterstock, Inc.; page 12, ©Jacek Chabraszewski/
Dreamstime.com; page 15, ©Lisa F. Young/Shutterstock, Inc.; page 17, ©Sefi
Greiver/Dreamstime.com; page 18, ©Kushal Bose/Shutterstock, Inc.; page 20,
©Kippy Spilker/Dreamstime.com; page 21, ©Saskia Massink/Dreamstime.com;
page 22, ©Ifeelstock/Dreamstime.com; page 27, ©Denis Pepin/Dreamstime.
com; page 28, ©Diego Vito Cervo/Dreamstime.com

Library of Congress Cataloging-in-Publication Data
Fontichiaro, Kristin.
  Know what to ask : forming great research questions /
by Kristin Fontichiaro and Emily Johnson.
      p. cm. — (Information explorer)
  Includes bibliographical references and index.
  ISBN 978-1-61080-483-7 (lib. bdg.) — ISBN 978-1-61080-570-4 (e-book) —
ISBN 978-1-61080-657-2 (pbk.)
  1. Research—Methodology—Juvenile literature. 2. Questioning—Juvenile
literature. I. Johnson, Emily, 1984– II. Title.
   ZA3080.F66 2012   2012008618
   001.4'2—dc23

Cherry Lake Publishing would like to acknowledge
the work of The Partnership for 21st Century Skills.
Please visit www.21stcenturyskills.org for more information.

Printed in the United States of America
Corporate Graphics Inc.
July 2012
CLFA11

Table of Contents

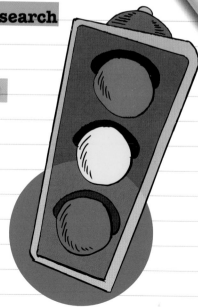

CHAPTER ONE
Questions Make the World Work

You have to ask the right questions to get the right answers.

Have you ever looked up at the sky and wondered why it's blue? Have you ever wondered how cars work? Have you ever been curious how your country was formed? Everyone has questions. We are constantly surrounded by things that we may not fully under-stand. We have questions about why things are the way they are. We look at the world around us and want to understand how it works.

We ask questions for a lot of different reasons, such as learning about the past, imagining the future, or solving a problem.

Where would we be if no one had ever asked, "Is there a better way to travel than by horse?" Or "Is there a way that computers could talk to each other?" Or "Could we use our TV to play games?" Those questions have all been answered, which is why we now have cars, the Internet, and video games. Some questions are still unanswered, such as "Why do people get old?" and "Why did *Triceratops* have three horns when other dinosaurs didn't?"

If no one ever asked questions, video games would never have been invented!

Some questions have easy answers. It's not hard to find the answer to a question like "Who was the first president of the United States?" The answer is a simple fact: George Washington.

Some questions take a lot more time to figure out, such as "What is the history of baseball?" You can't answer that with a single fact. To get a great answer, you might need to start by reading an **encyclopedia** to learn some basic facts about baseball, including who and what were some of the most important players, teams, and events. That's a start, but it would be more fun to

- interview some former baseball players;
- visit the Baseball Hall of Fame;
- read some books;
- check out some Major League Baseball Web sites;
- watch some **documentaries**; or
- go to a few games.

There is a lot we can learn about the history of baseball.

You could definitely learn more about the history of baseball if you did those things, and it would be fun! When we're really curious about something, we're willing to keep digging and learning!

Whether you're at home, at play, or at school, questioning is what makes the world around you work!

TRY THIS!

Set a timer for 1 minute. How many questions can you write down? When your minute is up,

- put a star next to the questions that you think you could answer by looking online;
- put a triangle next to those that you think a book could answer;
- put a smiley face next to those that you think an expert could answer; and
- put a question mark next to the questions you think have never been answered!

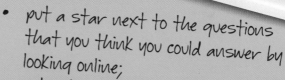

To get a copy of this activity, visit www.cherrylakepublishing.com/activities.

CHAPTER TWO
This Question Is Closed!

↑ Asking whether or not it is raining outside
will not get you very much information.

Some questions may have easy-to-find answers or only
one answer. We call these closed questions. Some examples of closed questions are:

- "What time is lunch?"
- "Where did I put my coat?"
- "Is it raining right now?"

Closed questions can usually be answered with "yes," "no," just a few words, or a single fact. For example, the question "What time is lunch?" has only one answer in your classroom. Lunch is either at 10:30 or 11:42 or 12:00, but there's only one right answer. "Where did I put my coat?" has only one correct answer, too. Sometimes, we call these red-light questions. Just like a red traffic light tells cars to stop, a red-light question is one where your questioning stops as soon as you find the answer.

Think back to the question in Chapter One, "Who was the first president of the United States?" That's a red-light question. As soon as you answer "George Washington," you're done. Red light! STOP!

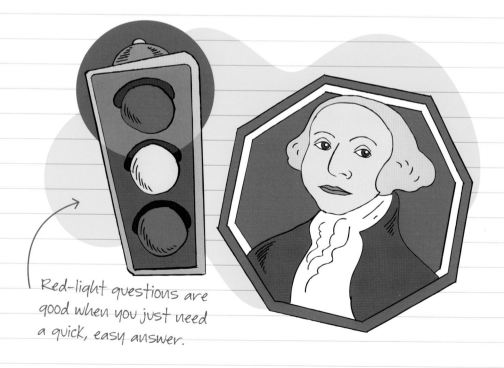

Red-light questions are good when you just need a quick, easy answer.

Sentences that start with **what**, **where**, or **when** tend to be red-light, closed questions. Sometimes, closed questions start with **how much** or **how many**. Not all questions follow this pattern, but most do! For example:

- **When** did the *Mayflower* land at Plymouth Rock? 1620
- **Where** did Grandma grow up? Italy
- **What** were the names of Christopher Columbus's three ships? The *Niña*, the *Pinta*, and the *Santa María*

Closed questions can be very helpful at times. They are important beginning steps to asking better questions. But when all you ask are red-light questions, you stop yourself from being curious about the world.

TRY THIS!

Imagine that an alien has just landed in your school's parking lot. The alien doesn't know anything about this strange building or its people. Imagine 10 closed questions that the alien might ask when he lands. Trade your questions with a friend. Are all of your questions closed? Can you answer the alien's questions easily? Try it!

To get a copy of this activity, visit www.cherrylakepublishing.com/activities.

CHAPTER THREE
Open for Business

Do you think it is odd that thunder doesn't usually make noise until after you've seen a lightning bolt?

In the last chapter, we talked about closed questions, questions with one right answer. There are other types of questions that may not be so easy to answer. They are usually a lot more interesting than closed questions! These types of questions will take more effort to answer.

Think about this question: Why do we see lightning before we hear thunder?

Can we answer that question with just a couple of words? No way! It would probably take a while to explain the answers to those questions. If we asked an

expert—such as a scientist—about it, she would probably need a few minutes to talk about how sound and
light travel and how storms form. Interesting stuff!

Questions that can't be answered simply are called
open-ended questions, because the answers are made
up of more than one piece of information. Again, like
traffic lights, these are green-light questions. Green
means go. When you get one piece of information, you
keep going. Green light—keep traveling! Keep looking
for more information.

Think about the question, "How would life be different if all the fresh water in the world dried up?"

What would happen if there was no more water
for us to drink?

The world would be a very different place without water.

Can you answer with "yes," "no," or "12:00"? No way! The answer is much more complicated. Here are some answers to what would happen:

- Plants would stop growing.
- Dogs would become thirsty and pant.
- We could not travel by boat or canoe.
- Lawns would dry up.
- People couldn't make lemonade.
- Nobody could do their laundry.

You probably have other answers, too. Because there is so much information that works together to answer the question, that's a sign of an open-ended, or green-light, question.

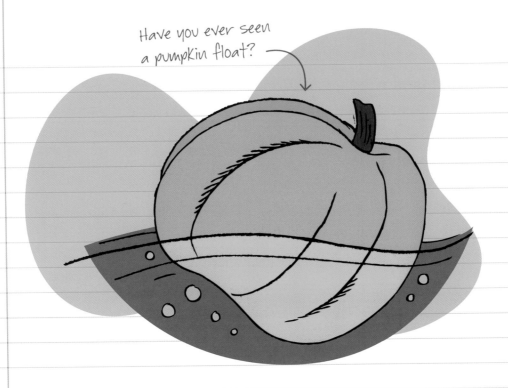

Have you ever seen a pumpkin float?

Open-ended questions usually—but don't always—start with **how** or **why**. Here are some examples:

- **How** does water turn into ice?
- **Why** do pumpkins float?
- **Why** did the American Civil War start?
- **How** was Utah settled?
- **How** did Andrew Jackson become president of the United States?

Open-ended questions are harder to answer. They may take more time. You will probably need to look at more than one book or Web site to see all the possible answers. You may have to get help from other people. Learning how to ask good open-ended questions will help you understand how to find the answers you're looking for.

This is where questioning turns into **research**. When we research, we ask questions and we look for answers. You probably do research at school, but some people keep doing research their whole lives. Lawyers, professors, scientists, inventors, and reporters do research all the time. They go online and use libraries, studios, newsrooms, or laboratories.

Professional athletes do research, too. They ask questions like "Why am I not hitting enough home runs?" They have coaches who help them watch videos of themselves, and they practice until they figure out an answer. Research is everywhere!

Have you ever had to do research for a school project?

TRY THIS!

Divide a piece of paper into two columns. Label the first column "Red-Light Questions" and the second "Green-Light Questions." In the first column, write five red-light questions. Have a friend do the same thing. Trade lists. Can you turn their red-light questions into green-light ones?

Take a look at these examples:

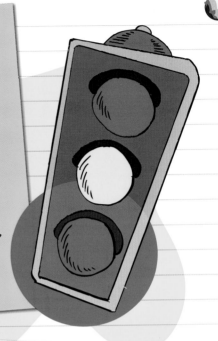

Red-Light Questions	Green-Light Questions
What is Massachusetts's Major League Baseball team?	What is the history of the Boston Red Sox?
How many flavors are there in Neapolitan ice cream?	How is ice cream made?

To get a copy of this activity, visit www.cherrylakepublishing.com/activities.

CHAPTER FOUR

Pre-Search Before Research

Have you ever seen a bush baby at a zoo?

Quick—what questions do you have about bush babies?
How about Demetrios Ypsilantis? Your questions are
probably "What's a bush baby?" and "Who is Demetrios
Ypsilantis?" Those are both closed questions, but that's
all we can ask because we don't know anything about
the topics. That happens a lot in school. Sometimes we

Austin is one of the biggest cities in Texas.

can't ask great questions because we don't know anything about what we're researching.

Let's pretend that you are going on vacation this
summer, but your parents can't decide where to go. They
are trying to decide between Texas and Michigan. They
also think it might be fun to simply visit another part
of your own state. They want you to do some research
on the places you could visit and the different activities
that are available in each place. Where should you start?
Well, it's always best to start with what you know.

For each state, make a list of things you already know. You probably know a lot about your own state. You've likely studied it in school or looked at it on a map. But imagine that you don't know much about Michigan. You might have a short list, like this:

What I Think I Know About Michigan	Questions I Have	What I've Learned
• shaped like a mitten • divided into two parts • capital is Lansing • Mariposa's dad lives there	• Are the two parts of the state connected? • What fun things can we do in the state?	

Is that enough for a report? Not yet. But it is definitely a good start. It is pretty interesting that Michigan is divided into two parts and shaped like a mitten. And it's always good to know where a state's capital is. And if Mariposa's dad lives there, maybe he could tell you some things.

There's another great way to start learning when you get stuck on what questions to ask: do some pre-search. When we pre-search, we're telling ourselves, "Hmmm. Before I go searching for details online or in books, I want to know some basics about my topic."

Michigan is home to many beautiful sights.

An encyclopedia is sure to have information about almost any topic you can think of.

One great way to pre-search is to use **encyclopedias**. In a lot of libraries, encyclopedias are sets of books that can take up a foot or more of shelf space. Inside, there is a little bit of information about a lot of different topics: plants, animals, places, people, and history. Many libraries also pay for encyclopedias that you can access online. These are great places to start. The information in encyclopedias is written by experts, so it is very reliable. It also gives you a general overview of the topic, so you can learn enough to ask questions. Ask your librarian for these common encyclopedia brands: World Book, Heinemann First Encyclopedia, Encyclopaedia Britannica, or Grolier Online.

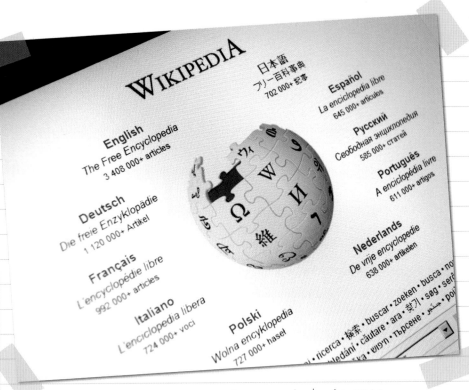

Wikipedia can be a useful place to begin your investigation.

Wikipedia, the biggest encyclopedia in the world, is not written just by experts. Almost anyone can edit it. That's both good and bad. Anybody can contribute, so Wikipedia is a huge collection of information about almost anything. On the other hand, because anybody can change the content, some information might be inaccurate. Smart researchers always use other sources after starting with Wikipedia or other online resources to be sure the information is accurate.

If we look up Michigan in an encyclopedia, we can get a lot of basic information fast. Now our list looks like this:

What I Think I Know About Michigan	Questions I Have	What I've Learned
• shaped like a mitten	• Are the two parts of the state connected?	
• divided into two parts	• Why does Michigan have so many sports teams?	
• capital is Lansing	• Why is the auto industry struggling?	
• Mariposa's dad lives there	• What kinds of cars do they make there?	
• center of struggling U.S. auto industry	• Why does Michigan have so many universities?	
• lots of farms—apples, cherries	• How would we get there from our house?	
• lots of universities and colleges	• Which players made the biggest contributions to the Tigers? Why?	
• lots of sports: Detroit Tigers, Red Wings, Pistons, Lions	• What fun things can we do in the state?	

See how many more questions we have now that we know a few more facts? A few minutes of reading an encyclopedia entry can really get you excited about your topic.

Here are tips for how to use any encyclopedia well:
- Use encyclopedias at the beginning of your questioning only.
- Use the section headings and the outline at the beginning to help you skim, or quickly read, the article.

- Look for basic facts and gather keywords you can use when you research with books, Web sites, or experts.
- Make notes about what you have learned.
- Write down new questions as they come up.

- Look at the very bottom of the entry. You might see references or external links. Click on those links, or type the addresses into your Web browser. You'll be able to see the articles or Web pages about the topic that someone else already decided are reliable and useful. That's better than typing your topic into a search engine!

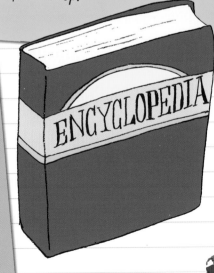

24

Once you've gotten that basic information, you don't need Wikipedia or any other encyclopedia anymore. Move on to meatier and more interesting articles, Web pages, books, or people!

What I Think I Know	Questions I Have	What I've Learned

TRY THIS!

Fold a large piece of paper in thirds. Make a chart with three columns like the one shown above. Pick a topic you don't know very much about. Brainstorm a list of what you think you know and what questions you have. Then read an encyclopedia entry about that topic. Brainstorm a new list of things you know and compare it to the old one to see how much you've learned!

To get a copy of this activity, visit www.cherrylakepublishing.com/activities.

CHAPTER FIVE
Any More Questions?

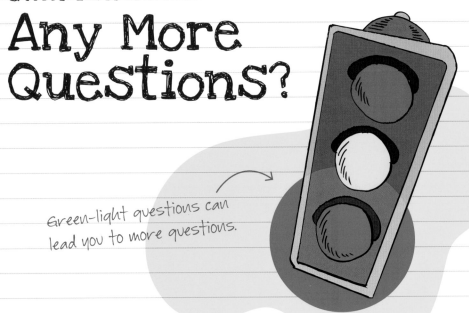

Green-light questions can lead you to more questions.

Now that we've researched different options, we're done, right? Nope! Once you think you've answered the question you asked, you need to **evaluate** your answer. This means you need to look at the question you asked, compare it to the answers you found, and decide whether that information has answered the question or led you to new questions.

When you evaluate your answers, you will usually find new questions that you weren't even aware of! For example, early on in your research about Michigan for your family trip, you might have wondered, "Are there ski resorts there?" Your family loves to downhill ski in the winter. But that would have been a closed question. You may have searched online for "Michigan ski resorts"

and discovered that there are both downhill and cross-country ski resorts in Michigan. This might have led to new questions. Maybe you asked yourself, "What's cross-country skiing?" and started a new search. Maybe you asked your parents, "Do you like to cross-country ski? Would you like to learn, or would you rather go downhill skiing?" Or you might have called a cross-country ski resort and asked, "Do you make artificial snow if we plan a trip and it doesn't snow? How do you do that?"

Good questions usually lead you to more questions, which lead you to more learning and exploration. That doesn't mean you goofed up on your questions. It means you are really interested in your topic!

What kind of skiing would you like to try?

Thomas Edison asked the right questions to keep us out of the dark!

Sometimes, though, we get stumped, and our questions seem to have no answers. If that happens, try adding **synonyms**, or words that mean the same as your keywords. If you are stumped when searching for "ski resorts," try "ski companies" or "ski hills." Still stumped? Try searching for "ski equipment." If you can find a ski store, there is probably a snowy hill nearby. Call and ask!

Remember, all over the world, some questions are still waiting to be answered. Think about scientists or experts. Their job is to ask questions, all day every day! Imagine if Thomas Edison had never wondered how to make electricity into a light. Many people wondered if it was possible, but it was Edison's curiosity that turned a question into an answer. What if Columbus had never wondered if there was another way to sail around the world? Many of our ancestors might never have come to North America.

Questioning is not a once-in-a-while activity for most people. When we learn to ask great questions, we are building skills that we can use for the rest of our lives. We are learning new things and exploring the world around us.

TRY THIS!

Let's put everything we've talked about into practice! Get a small notebook and, before you go to bed at night, write down every question you can think of that came up during the day. You can also carry the notebook with you and write your questions down as soon as they come to mind. When you find an answer, write it down. Create your own personal encyclopedia. And who knows— maybe your questions will lead you to the next big discovery!

MY NOTEBOOK

To get a copy of this activity, visit www.cherrylakepublishing.com/activities.

Glossary

documentaries (dahk-yuh-MEN-tur-eez) films that are about real facts, people, and events

encyclopedias (en-sye-kloh-PEE-dee-uhz) books or sets of books with information on a wide variety of topics

evaluate (i-VAL-yoo-ate) decide the importance of something by thinking about it carefully

keywords (KEE-wurdz) words that can be uses to search for information on Web sites

outline (OUT-line) a quick list of the most important ideas in a paper or article

references (REF-ruhn-siz) the Web sites, articles, books, and other materials that a writer uses to write a report

research (REE-surch) the process of asking questions, finding answers, and evaluating those answers

section headings (SEK-shuhn HED-ingz) bold print that tells the main idea of the paragraphs about to be read

synonyms (SIN-uh-nimz) words that share a meaning

Find Out More

BOOKS

Rabbat, Suzy. *Find Your Way Online*. Ann Arbor, MI: Cherry
 Lake Publishing, 2010.

Truesdell, Ann. *Find the Right Site*. Ann Arbor, MI: Cherry Lake
 Publishing, 2010.

Truesdell, Ann. *Fire Away: Asking Great Interview Questions*.
 Ann Arbor, MI: Cherry Lake Publishing, 2013.

WEB SITES

Fact Monster

www.factmonster.com

This free, ad-supported site features an almanac, atlas, encyclopedia, dictionary, and thesaurus. It's recommended for kids
ages 8 to 14 as a pre-search site.

Google Search Education Evangelism

https://sites.google.com/site/gwebsearcheducation/

This site offers a set of lessons and strategies for learning to be
a better online searcher.

The Kentucky Virtual Library Presents: How to Do Research

www.kyvl.org/kids/homebase.html

A research map helps guide students through the process of
research, by suggesting questions, what you already know, and
keywords.

Index

Kristin Fontichiaro teaches at the University of Michigan, where scholars, professors, students, and scientists are always asking questions!

About the Authors

Emily Johnson was born in Utah, went to school in Michigan, and is now the librarian at Pledge Harbor School in Dhaka, the capital city of Bangladesh. As she travels the world, she asks lots of questions!